for Prism
Premiered November 19, 2004 at Symphony Space, New York

Scherzino

Tenor Saxophone in B♭

WILLIAM BOLCOM
2004

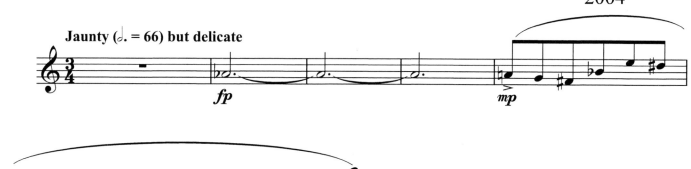

*trattenuto = just slightly held back

Tenor Saxophone in B♭

Scherzino

WILLIAM BOLCOM

Tenor Saxophone in B♭

G.P.
(in time)